£7.99

A Pillar Box Red Publication

© 2013. Published by Pillar Box Red Publishing Ltd.

ISBN 978-1-907823-65-7

Images © Corbis.com and Shutterstock.com

we ♥ love you...

JLS

FAREWELL SOUVENIR EDITION

A 2014 ANNUAL

Written by Becky Bowden

Designed by Lucy Boyd

CONTENTS

A Fond Farewell

On 24 April 2013 JLS announced their decision to split, following a final Goodbye tour. The Greatest Hits tour is scheduled for December 2013 and set to be a sell-out event, making it the biggest and best send-off to JLS possible as the boys bow out of the entertainment industry as a group.

The news broke fast, taking the entertainment world by storm and leaving fans of JLS completely shocked by this sudden and unexpected news. Whilst it may have seemed like a spur of the moment decision, the band insist that it was a tough call to make and that they would rather go out on a high point in their career. Aston spoke out to The Sun newspaper, saying:

"The question was asked, 'Can you do this together for another five or so years? Can you see that happening?' Between the four of us, there was no definite 'Yes' in the room. We had to dig deep and find the right solution. We haven't fallen out. We leave with some amazing successes under our belt and we can say goodbye in style."

Oritsé added how the band's split will affect not only the fans and JLS in general but also their families who have all become close throughout their career together. He said:

"There's nothing more I love than performing with the rest of the boys. It's been a massive part of my life and my family's life, especially with my mum. She treats the boys as if they are her sons. Hopefully, we can make sure it's going to be the biggest celebration on that last date, especially because it's going to be the last time that anybody is going to see us together on stage."

JLS also said the following via their website and in interviews regarding their decision to split:

NEWS

"We wanted to make sure that you heard it from the four of us that we have decided to bring our time as a band to an end. Goodbye; The Greatest Hits Tour will be the last time that we will perform together as a four and we want to make sure that this tour is the best ever and that we end on a high!

"We will always remain brothers and friends and we will always be your boys. Thanks to all of you guys, your support, your dedication and you have changed our lives forever. We wouldn't be where we are today without you."

"As always we will continue to support each other and we hope you will enjoy watching us grow individually in our new chapters going forward.

"We want to look at this final year as a celebration of all that we have achieved together. We hope you can look back and remember all the great moments that you have been responsible for."

J.B. later tweeted several messages to fans, including: "I also know you will all take this in different ways but we will always be there for you guys even though we are no longer a group!! J x.

"Roll on the greatest hits tour!! The next chapter has begun, watch this space...hehe J x."

ALAN CARR

LOUIS TOMLINSON

OLLY MURS

Emotional Oritsé

Oritsé got emotional when he broke down on 'Alan Carr: Chatty Man' the TV show during the band's interview about their decision to split.

J.B. told Alan Carr and the audience: "It's Oritsé's baby effectively, you know. He brought us together. It's an emotional decision. "

As Oritsé broke down in tears in front of their host and the crowd, clearly being hit by a wave of sudden emotion, Marvin stepped in to elaborate further by saying:

"We're best friends, we're brothers, the bond between us is indescribable. We've been through so much since we first came together and no one would have dreamed what we achieved could be possible, and of course for it to all end was a massively emotional decision, and it wasn't one that was taken lightly."

Celebrities React to JLS Split Announcement!

JLS have lots of celebrity friends and fans, so it was no surprise that they took to social networking websites like Twitter to air their own thoughts on the breaking news.

One Direction's Louis Tomlinson tweeted: "Sad to hear about JLS. Wish them all the best of luck in what they go on to do."

The ever funny Simon Pegg commented: "Is it true DFS is closing down?! Sorry, JLS. So are JLS having a closing down sale?"

Olly Murs tweeted: "Gutted to hear about @ JLSOfficial splitting up! 4 top lads.. I'll never forget the prank, the tunes, the tour, simply a class boyband!"

KATY BRAND

LYDIA BRIGHT

RONAN KEATING

LAURA WHITMORE

NATHAN SYKES

Katy Brand: "I think the writing was sort of on the wall for #JLS when J.B. turned up on Countryfile last week saying he was going to become a farmer..."

Laura Whitmore commented: "JLS are splitting??? Whaaa.. Didn't see that one coming. Maybe they can be on next year's Big reunion show??"

Rochelle tweeted about her husband and the JLS lads with a heartfelt message saying: "As well as being a wife I'm a big @JLSOfficial fan. I am V sad its the end of an era. What an amazing run. I'm so proud. Roll on the tour x I'm so so proud of them. 4 genuine best friends."

Nathan Sykes from The Wanted said: "Sad to hear about @JLSOfficial. Some of the nicest guys in the business. Good luck to them all in the future! :)"

Antony Costa from Blue tweeted: "Morning all.. just woke up to the news that @JLSOfficial have split..really gutted.. good luck to them all in whatever they do #toplads"

Former Towie star Mark Wright had a tearful response, saying: "Not gonna lie, my eyes watered a little bit reading that @JLSOfficial are splitting. Sad article. Congrats to all your success boys #bigfan"

Mark Wright's pal and ex TOWIE star Lydia Bright also said: "Nooooooo JLS have split, I'm so shocked"

Ronan Keating tweeted: "Just heard the news about @JLSOfficial. Wish the boys the best in whatever it is they roll on too. They had a great run."

The Rise to Fame

Since 2008, the name JLS has sat firmly on the lips of the great British public and indeed the rest of the world. Their blend of soulful vocals, catchy pop tunes and impressive dance moves has seen this four piece boy band achieve star status in just a few years. A rare achievement in today's fast-paced music industry.

The band first signed to Tracklacers production company New Track City under their original name 'UFO' before shooting straight to fame on ITV's the X Factor in 2008 with a fresh sounding new title. The change came after it was revealed that their original name was already in use by another group. So JLS was chosen, short for Jack the Lad Swing, a style of music the band was using at the time! Imagine a world where JLS never existed and if all of the hits we now know them for were by 'UFO' instead!

The name JLS suited the band perfectly however, and soon proved to be just as popular with the general public as it was with the boys themselves, with everyone being keen to show their support to the new and modern sounding group, who were already showing all the signs of having that perfect star quality.

JLS is made up of four fantastic band members. They are of course: Oritsé Williams, Marvin Humes, Aston Merrygold and J.B. Gill. It was Oritsé himself who originally started putting a band together. He had been scouted for many different boy bands up until that point but he seemed to be looking for more of a personal connection with a group. The band gathered its members slowly and through personal connections and recommendations, forming strong bonds and genuine friendships with one another along the way. Maybe this is the key to their hugely successful career and chart topping success as a unified group? If so, it certainly seems to have paid off.

During their X Factor experience, JLS were mentored by Louis Walsh and made it to the nail-biting final stages of the competition, coming second only to Alexandra Burke after the public chose her version of the winners' song 'Hallelujah' as their final winning act.

It was reported that Simon Cowell was so impressed by the band that he offered them a recording contract with his record company 'Syco' for a substantial advance payment. However, it was later revealed that Cowell had changed his mind, reportedly in order to focus

With a series of hit singles and successful albums continuously appearing, there seemed to be no stopping JLS as they received worldwide attention from loyal fans and airplay on every radio station imaginable.

Throughout their fast and incredibly furious career, the boys have seen their lives change in unimaginable ways, with their fans always supporting and encouraging them from the wings. From sell-out concerts to TV appearances, the boys could do no wrong and managed to avoid the mistakes and downfalls of pop stars past. However, all good things must eventually come to an end, and for JLS that moment came on 24 April 2013 when they took to their official website and released a statement announcing that they would be splitting up, after releasing their greatest hits collection and embarking on a third and final arena tour.

more time and attention on developing the career of Alexandra Burke. This was merely a bump in the road for a clearly talented JLS though; as shortly after, they went on to sign a recording contract with Epic Records in 2009.

Things moved incredibly quickly in JLS' career after that point. They were put in touch with some of the best producers and song writers of the moment in the pop industry and it was then that their first single 'Beat Again' was born and released, all within the space of roughly a month.

'Beat Again' amazed everyone by reaching number 1 in the UK singles chart on 19th of July 2009. This was it, JLS were officially big news, and their fan base was unstoppable! The UK hadn't seen a band this successful in years and JLS were set to reap their own rewards.

The band's close knit bond and hardworking ethics meant that they thrived in the entertainment industry in a way that many acts before them had failed to do. They weren't just living the pop star dream, they were re-creating it as they went, pushing boundaries and proving those who ever doubted them to be 100% wrong!

The statement was met with a general reaction of shock and disappointment but as one of the UK's best loved acts, their final tour and album are set to be one emotional and heartfelt goodbye to a classic, successful pop band. Let's hope they go out on the high note that they deserve!

SPOTLIGHT ON...
ASTON

Name:	Aston Merrygold
Birthday:	February 13th 1988
Star Sign:	Aquarius
Eye Colour:	Brown
Favourite Colour:	Blue
Favourite Food:	Pasta or pizza
Favourite Artists:	Usher, Mario, Michael Jackson, Beyonce, Chris Brown, Boyz II Men
Favourite Films:	Favourite films - Rush Hour, Rush Hour 2, Rush Hour 3, Bad Boy, Bad Boys 2, You Got Served, Stomp The Yard, Taken, The Pursuit Of Happyness
Likes:	Fast cars, football, LA, producing music
Dislikes:	Big dogs!

SPOTLIGHT ON...
ORITSÉ

Name:	Oritsé Williams
Birthday:	November 27th 1986
Star Sign:	Sagittarius
Eye Colour:	Hazel
Favourite Artists:	Tina Turner, Stevie Wonder, Prince, Michael Jackson, Lenny Kravitz, Usher, Musiq Soulchild, Aretha Franklin, India Arie, John Legend
Favourite Films:	The Lion King, The Pursuit Of Happyness, Sister Act, The Temptations, Shawshank Redemption, You Got Served, Notorious, X-Men, Ray, Dream Girls, Alfie
Favourite Colour:	Red
Favourite Food:	Anything at Nando's
Likes:	Music, great food and family
Dislikes:	Vertical theme park rides and maths!

SPOTLIGHT ON...

J.B.

Name:	Jonathan Benjamin Gill
Birthday:	December 7th 1986
Star Sign:	Sagittarius
Eye Colour:	Brown
Favourite Artists:	Michael Jackson, Beyonce, Lionel Richie
Favourite Films:	Training Day, Bad Boys 2, American Gangster, Gladiator, Coming 2 America, The Pursuit Of Happyness, Crash
Favourite Colour:	Yellow
Favourite Food:	Chinese
Likes:	Family time, farming, rugby
Dislikes:	Snakes!

SPOTLIGHT ON...

MARVIN

Name:	Marvin Humes
Birthday:	March 18th 1985
Star Sign:	Pisces
Eye Colour:	Brown
Favourite Artists:	Michael Jackson, Marvin Gaye, Stevie Wonder, Usher, Ne-Yo, Mariah Carey, Prince, Boyz II Men, Justin Timberlake, Craig David
Favourite Films:	The Goonies, Back To The Future, The Matrix, Titanic, Donnie Brasco, Seven, Scarface, Cruel Intentions, Legends Of The Falls, Moon Walker
Favourite Colour:	Green
Favourite Food:	Nando's chicken
Likes:	Football, DJ'ing and spending time with his wife and daughter
Dislikes:	Spiders!

LIVE ON STAGE

Wedding Bells and Babies

Love has certainly been in the air for the JLS boys during the past few years of their fast-paced career! With all of them havin received much media attention for their love-lives, it has been Marvin who has been mostly in the spotlight, due to a high profil romance with The Saturday's band member Rochelle Wiseman.

The two have enjoyed a rollercoaster romance that has seen them go from loved up and dating, to an engagement on 31 December 2011 where Marvin popped the question in the Maldives, and then finally on to marriage when the couple tied the knot at the luxurious Blenheim Palace on 27 July 2012.

Their wedding was kept closely under wraps but a few of the details did emerge shortly afterwards. For instance, we know that Rochelle wore a Vera Wang wedding dress a she told OK Magazine:

"It had to be Vera Wang. Marvin proposed two days into a ten-day holiday and I was itching to get back so I could go and find my dress. To me, Vera Wang's designs are the ultimate. I knew I'd find my dream dress in her collection and I did."

Marvin was joined by the rest of his bandmates of course, who all showed up looking very dapper for their best friend's big day. As you'd expect, there were also quite a few famous faces in attendance such as Girls Aloud's Nicola Roberts, Simon Webbe from Blue, Harry Styles, Liam Payne and Niall Horan of One Direction, Tulisa Contostavlos, hit singers Olly Murs, Pixie Lott and rappers Chipmunk and Wretch 32. Wow, what a list!

There was much more happiness to come for the couple when on 20th of May 2013, Rochelle gave birth to their first child, a daughter named Alaia-Mai. With a loving family and some seriously stylish influences from the band and her parents, we're sure that little Alaia-Mai will be a mini style icon herself in no time!

CHIPMUNK

HARRY STYLES

NICOLA ROBERTS

PIXIE LOTT

Awards & Recognition

BRIT Awards

Date	Award	Type
2010	British Group	Nominees
2010	British Single: 'Beat Again'	Winners
2010	British Breakthrough	Winners
2012	British Single: 'She Makes Me Wanna'	Nominees

MOBO Awards

Date	Award	Type
2009	Best UK Newcomer	Winners
2009	Best Song: 'Beat Again'	Winners
2010	Best UK Act	Winners
2010	Best Album: 'JLS'	Winners
2012	Best Video: 'Do You Feel What I Feel'	Winners

Arriving at the BRIT Awards 201 Nominations at the Savoy Hotel, London

JLS arrive at the MOBO Awards 2012
at the Liverpool Echo Arena

World Music Awards

Date	Award	Type
2012	World's Best Group	Nominees

Virgin Media Awards

Date	Award	Type
2009	Best Group	Nominees
2009	Best Newcomer	Nominees
2009	Best Track: 'Beat Again'	Nominees
2009	Hottest Male: Aston Merrygold	Nominees
2013	Best Group	Nominees

BT Digital Music Awards

Date	Award	Type
2010	Best Group	Winners
2010	Best Video: 'Everybody In Love'	Winners
2011	Best Group	Winners
2011	Best Video: 'Eyes Wide Shut'	Winners
2011	Best Fan site: 'Eyes Wide Shut'	Nominees

Spot the Difference

There are 8 differences in the pictures below. Can you spot them?

Answers on page 60

Desert Island Demands

Ever thought about what you would take with you if you were stuck on a desert island? The boys have, but can you match what three items each member chose out of the selection below?

Answers on page 60

THE BEST BITS

With the news of JLS splitting up, fans have been focusing on the band's amazing career rather than dwelling on their demise. JLS have had some amazing career highlights over the years; let's take a look at some of the biggest and best moments in JLS history!

THE X FACTOR

Without the X Factor JLS might not have become the massive musical stars they are today. The show catapulted them to the forefront of the public eye and was, without doubt, a great way to kick-start their music career. Having been mentored by Louis Walsh and championed by Simon Cowell as one of the best acts in the competition all the way through, they may have missed out on winning the competition but that didn't stop them from achieving worldwide success in the music and entertainment industry.

Coming second only to Alexandra Burke in the X Factor meant that JLS were a firm favourite with the public right until the very end of the final show, giving us plenty of time to witness their fun personalities and versatile performances on stage. Always upbeat and positive and providing viewers with constant entertainment means that when the band were ready to unleash themselves upon the music world, they had a readymade fan base waiting for them, one that continued to grow over the years that followed.

FIRST NUMBER ONE

A real defining moment for JLS was when their debut single Beat Again made it to number one, confirming the band's talent and making the UK really stand up and take notice of this hot new boy band that had emerged onto the scene!

'Beat Again' reached number one in the UK singles chart on 19th July 2009 and was followed by a self-titled album 'JLS' which also topped the charts, making its debut at the number one spot.

FAN SUPPORT

The JLS fans have been loyal and supportive to the band throughout their career. JLS are always appreciative and kind-natured to their fans, believing that their success is all down to their continued love and support. They addressed the fans personally when announcing their split on the official JLS website saying, "Thanks to all of you guys, your support, your dedication and your love, you have changed our lives forever and we wouldn't be where we are today without you." Some fans even set up a support group on social networking website Twitter to see each other through the band's break up.

JLS are well known for always taking time out of their busy schedule to visit their fans in hospital. They have made regular visits to Birmingham Children's Hospital and Great Ormond Street Hospital and taken the time to chat with their younger fans and to sign merchandise for them.

THE JLS FOUNDATION

The JLS Foundation was set up in 2010 in order to fund projects close to the band's hearts and raise money for a series of great causes. JLS were quoted as saying:

"We wanted to support causes that affect our young fans and invest in their futures".

(Source – jlsfoundation.co.uk)

It has been confirmed that the JLS Foundation will continue to run even after the band are no longer performing together as a group and shall continue giving support to many different charities including Rays of Sunshine, MS Society, Brook, NSPCC, Sport Relief and Beat Bullying. The fund has also begun supporting Cancer Research UK with the shared goal of raising two million pounds over two years to fund research into cancers affecting children, teenagers and young adults.

SELL-OUT TOURS AND TOP PERFORMANCES

All of JLS tours and appearances have been hugely popular, sell-out events. Some of them have seen fans spend hours in queues just to get hold of tickets, or in extreme cases even camping overnight to ensure that they get the very best view of their all-time favourite band! Now that's dedication.

One of JLS' top performances and the most notable to date had to be when they performed at the Queen's Diamond Jubilee concert. They took to the imposing stage outside Buckingham Palace and performed some of their best known tracks alongside a whole host of famous stars, sending the crowd wild!

CHILDREN IN NEED

JLS were heavily involved with the 2010 Children in Need event and their song 'Love You More' was even chosen to be the official Children in Need song for that year! 'Love You More' was then released on 14th November 2010 and became the band's fourth number one record.

The boys performed their track live on stage and really got into the fun-filled spirit that makes Children in Need so special.

REDONE COLLABORATION

JLS don't always like to do things the conventional way in the music industry. Instead of going down the average route in their quest to work with producers Swizz Beatz and RedOne, JLS reportedly decided to bid £30,000 in a charity auction raising money for the Keep a Child Alive charity.

This unconventional approach not only helped to raise an amazing amount of money at the event, which was being held by fellow musician Alicia Keys, but also resulted in the band teaming up with these high flying producers to release the track we now know as 'She Makes Me Wanna', which gave the JLS lads their fifth number one single! This is one of the many decisions taken by the band that have shown that not only are JLS dedicated to their careers and to working with some of the best industry insiders, but that they are always keen to put their money towards a fantastic cause in the process.

ALEXANDRA BURKE

LOUIS WALSH

REDONE

SWISS BEATZ

QUICKFIRE LYRICS QUIZ

So you think you know all the words to every JLS song?
Well put that to the test by guessing the missing lyrics.

1. Let's just get back together, we should have never broke up, they're telling me, that my heart won't beat again. We should've stayed together, * * * * * * *, they're telling me, my heart won't beat again.

2. You know you need someone, when the need's so strong, when they're gone you don't know how to go on, so the whole world is * * * *, standing still until they come back, you accept that they've, got things to do, but sometimes in the end there's nothing left for you, if hurt is missing your baby, I've done too muc it lately.

3. I need you, I need you in my life, nob nobody loves me like you, if there wa ****, to stop you from leaving, caus we're not through, if only tonight, if t is all I got, if I can't have your love, I won't get back up this time.

4. Gonna tell you how I feel , I hope tha I'm real, *****, yeah, now I'm so afr left it all too late, but won't you hear now though.

5. But even as I walk away, and I say I'm gonna stay, it only takes a ***, cause you and I both know the truth, I'm crazy for you, I'm crazy for you, I'm crazy for you.

6. Girl when you move it's a private show, got me wondering how low you can go, girl you the fire come and put that heat on me, don't tell your friends that ***, just push your way out through the crowd, meet me in the corner where nobody else can see.

7. Now she's taking me to a galaxy, and I can't believe I'm touching her, and she has me where ****, and I'm floating up off this earth.

8. It's not about the Louis or the Prada, she don't even bother, she can have it all but doesn't need it, she likes the *****, simple and beautiful, she ain't bout material, believe it.

9. I can move mountains, if that's what it takes, go supersonic, you'll never have to wait, my pulse is racing like crazy, whenever you're around, ****, before I shut this whole block down.

10. I just gotta step back, I don't wanna keep falling, don't wanna trade with your heart, cause you can't afford it!, don't wanna give up, find it ****, look deep inside that the love between us is growing.

11. Can you feel the temperature rising, do you feel the ****, let me cast a beat and we'll ride it, go ahead and put your hands up.

12. I try to send her shopping, she doesn't buy distractions, it's like my platinum declined, declined now, I think she started doubting, I better ***, I'm kinda reading bad sign, bad signs now.

13. But everybody knows how the story goes, something in your eyes said the innocence over now, telling me that you found somebody new, **** said the innocence over now, girl I really loved you more than I could tell you, something in the air said the innocence over now.

14. Mountains in my way, I can't lie, at times they seem too high, but I just climb, I told them that I won't stop 'til I reach the other side, they don't get to decide, no, *****.

15. Keep me alive, check my vital signs, my pulse feels weak, so weak, I need a supply of your mouth to mouth, don't speak, load me, don't speak, the flow of your ****, and let's go cause it's live or die we're chasing, oh.

Answers on page 61

Fashion Focus

JLS have always been one of the best-dressed pop groups. Their stylish looks have been a hit with fans and have earned them photo spreads in some of the world's best glossy magazines and paparazzi shots by those who are keen to keep up to date with what outfits the boys are wearing and what trends they're currently sporting.

Some of JLS' unique and fashionable style can be attributed to international celebrity stylist and bespoke fashion editor Mark McMahon. Mark began styling the group after their previous stylist Simon Foxton suggested him to the group just as their second album was being launched. Mark certainly helped to give the boys a more defined style and look.

The band is always spotted wearing modern trends that are right on key with the fashion movement at that time. They are lucky enough to be able to wear just about any style of clothing and still look great. We've seen them dressed up in their smart, sleek suits at award ceremonies or dressed down in bright, sporty outfits for more casual events. They are usually seen wearing fitted items of clothing that look immaculately tailored.

Oritsé is a big fan of hats, when speaking to GQ magazine in 2010, he told them, "I argue with stylists about hats. They have to be a certain kind of hat, at a certain angle, or else it won't work. The boys know."

J.B. isn't afraid to go for a smarter look and is often pictured wearing polo shirts and braces.

Their love of fashion has even seen JLS launch their own clothing range and their fragrance 'Kiss' which sold 100,000 bottles on its first day of release! It became the fastest-selling celebrity fragrance in twenty years and beat the likes of Madonna, Beyonce and Justin Bieber who have all released their own branded scents.

No doubt the JLS boys will all develop an even more versatile style as they continue down their solo career routes, and it will be interesting to see what each individual member steps out in when they're not being pictured alongside their fellow band mates.

Wordsearch

Can you spot the JLS-related words in the wordsearch below?
You can find all of the correct answers at the back, but no cheating!

Y	F	S	T	I	H	T	S	E	T	A	E	R	G	W	T	V	X	H
T	E	V	E	R	Y	B	O	D	Y	I	N	L	O	V	E	L	L	H
X	E	K	C	R	R	D	G	D	L	W	L	K	G	K	T	B	T	T
M	P	P	D	N	N	V	U	P	H	S	X	K	L	F	E	R	L	R
T	I	O	N	R	F	J	B	O	E	H	L	N	T	A	N	X	M	Z
J	C	K	R	W	A	L	M	M	R	F	H	U	T	V	N	D	B	H
X	B	C	W	I	R	W	U	T	R	P	H	A	E	B	J	L	Y	P
D	P	L	K	L	T	H	A	O	K	S	G	Y	P	C	T	R	H	P
X	J	H	Q	H	N	S	C	T	E	A	B	H	Y	V	U	O	B	D
L	Q	B	B	I	J	H	E	D	I	D	R	V	T	F	F	W	V	F
N	T	P	V	W	E	U	I	N	O	R	F	N	I	Q	O	S	B	K
F	C	R	J	L	C	W	K	O	T	C	B	L	R	M	T	I	M	Y
G	A	M	L	N	S	R	G	E	L	W	X	L	A	P	G	H	G	Y
M	W	E	Y	E	X	V	T	K	B	Y	B	I	H	G	P	T	B	T
N	W	X	Y	N	K	H	L	X	R	O	Z	G	C	G	N	A	V	H
M	T	E	X	Y	T	J	Y	J	W	N	X	B	F	M	L	T	H	X
D	R	B	H	V	T	Y	L	W	T	D	C	J	K	X	L	T	N	K
M	P	L	R	O	T	C	A	F	X	J	K	G	P	V	C	U	N	P
Q	A	S	T	O	N	E	V	O	L	U	T	I	O	N	F	O	J	N

JB GILL
MARVIN HUMES
ASTON
ORITSE
UFO
BEAT AGAIN
X FACTOR

BRIT AWARD
OUTTA THIS WORLD
GOODBYE
EVOLUTION
EVERYBODY IN LOVE
JUKEBOX

EPIC
ROCHELLE
GREATEST HITS
PROUD
CHARITY
EYES WIDE SHUT

Answers
on page
61

40

Who Bought What

They may be up there with some of their favourite artists these days, but can you guess who bought what for their first album purchase?

This album belongs to:

....

This album belongs to:

....

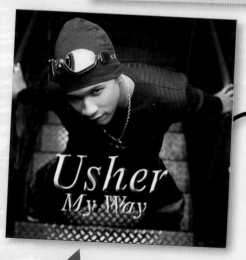

This album belongs to:

....

This album belongs to:

....

Answers on page 60

Showbiz Buddies

During their time in the entertainment industry JLS have become friends with some influential celebrities and have met and worked alongside many mega-stars!

The Saturdays

The Saturdays and JLS boys are great friends. They are all connected through Marvin from JLS and Rochelle from The Saturdays relationship and are regularly pictured out and about together. They stay in touch loads through Twitter and the girl band all donned their best outfits for Rochelle and Marvin's wedding. They are often working on the same events in the music industry and performing at the same gigs, such as Hyde Park in 2013. The two groups share a close relationship and we can't see that changing any time soon, even with JLS' recent split.

Rylan Clark

Things have been going really well for Rylan Clark since his time on The X Factor and Celebrity Big Brother! Not only has he performed in sell-out tours for his musical career but he's also bagged himself some fantastic presenting contracts, including working with Emma Willis presenting Big Brother's Bit on the Side!

The multi-talented 'love him or hate him' star has met the band on many occasions and was pictured enjoying a night out with Aston Merrygold in Manchester in January 2013 with some of their mutual friends.

Olly Murs

Olly Murs is a good friend of the band. These cheeky chaps have even been known to play the odd prank on one another, with JLS going all out in 2012 when they played a huge prank on Olly during a seemingly routine interview for a Stand Up To Cancer event.

Olly was supposed to fire Aston from a human cannon on to a safety mat, but unknown to him, Aston was replaced by a trained stuntman who deliberately missed the mat. Aston pretended to be injured, leaving Olly looking completely shocked and worried for his pal! When the trick was revealed, Olly looked shocked yet relieved that his friend was actually OK. He later took to Twitter and tweeted "Still recording, still shaking and still shocked!!" Followed by: "@JLSOfficial you got me proper today!!" Poor old Olly! What a crazy day.

Ben Foden

Ben Foden is a top rugby union footballer who plays for Northampton Saints and England. He is married to The Saturdays band member Una Healy and the couple have a daughter together named Aoife Belle Foden, born on March 13th 2012. Given JLS' close relationship with The Saturdays' girls, it's only natural that he's also become a good friend of the band.

JLS Mega Quiz

1. What does JLS stand for?

2. JLS were runners up in which season of the X Factor?

3. Who did they come second to?

4. Which single did JLS release for 2010 Comic Relief?

5. Which pop act did Oritsé write a song for?

6. What was the name of the song?

7. Which classic BBC TV show did Marvin appear in?

8. Who is Marvin Married to?

9. Which Christmas special did J.B. Gill win?

10. Where was Aston born?

11. Before the band settled on JLS they were called UFO, but what did it stand for?

12. Which artist featured on the band's 'Eyes Wide Shut' track?

13. What was the name of JLS` 2011 album?

14. What were JLS the first British music act to ever do?

15. What is the name of JLS and Alexandra Burke's clothing line?

16. What is the name of JLS` debut fragrance?

17. Which band member started the group?

18. Who is the youngest member of the band?

19. When did JLS split up?

20. What were JLS` first two singles?

Answers on page 61

45

SAY WHAT?

The JLS boys aren't exactly known for being shy and quiet in the entertainment industry. They are always professional and in great spirits during interviews and via social media networks and are happy to chat about their latest projects. Here are some of the best JLS quotes and tweets from recent years.

Top Tweets 2013

Oritse @Oritse 20 May
WOW the 1st baby of JLS . Congrats @MarvinHumes & @RochelleTheSats . Alaia-Mai Welcome to the big beautiful World! Love Uncle Reesh x

Marvin Humes @MarvinHumes 20 May
This morning we welcomed our baby girl Alaia-Mai Humes..Mum is doing great & baby is amazing! We are both overjoyed! Thanks for your love x

JLS @JLSOfficial 30 Mar
Weddings are such beautiful occasions!!congratulations Rachael and Jonathan!!lots of love J x

JLS @JLSOfficial 16 Apr
Guys I hav learnt of the tragic recent events in Boston & encourage the World to come together & support #PrayForBoston

JLS @JLSOfficial 29 Mar
Wow wow wow..What an incredible feeling..You guys make me so happy thank you for all the love and support tonight it means the world! Marv x

JLS @JLSOfficial 21 Mar
Baseline... Girls like my... Baseline... Girls like my... Bassline.. Shake it to my gon make it to my get but naked to my! #cartunes Ax

JLS @JLSOfficial 24 Apr
JLSters, I'll forever be thankful for all you've done..we have to draw the positives from a sad time..it's been amazing!I love u all..Marv x

JLS @JLSOfficial 20 Mar
I hate when you wake up with a really good interesting tweet...then u get showered and ready and forget what you wanted to say! #annoying Jx

JLS @JLSOfficial 19 Apr
jus got home!! someone please put me in the next Avengers Assemble Movie, i'd be any superhero thats available!! #HYPPEDDD ORI X

JLS @JLSOfficial 24 Apr
To our wonderfully heart felt fans, we've shared a phenomenal 5 years with you, memories that will never fade. Love you 4ever More! Ori♥♥♥♥

Cool Quotes

Speaking on Alan Carr Chatty Man about their decision to split:

J.B. started the conversation by saying: 'It's Oritsé's baby effectively, you know. He brought us together."

Marvin continued: "It's an emotional decision. We're best friends, we're brothers, the bond between us is indescribable.

"We've been through so much since we first came together and no one would have dreamed what we achieved could be possible.

"And of course for it to all end was a massively emotional decision, and it wasn't one that was taken lightly."

Marvin also explained: "We've had an incredible career for five years and we want to see it as a celebration that we've achieved so much."

"We wanted to go out on top and not be that act where people are like, 'Oh bloody hell, it's JLS again'."

Oritsé speaks about the fans in an interview on digitalspy.co.uk saying:

"We have amazing fans - we love them following us wherever we go. They get really stuck in and support us, so to win it would be amazing not only for us, but everyone that's involved in JLS."

Marvin Humes spoke to MTV in 2013 with some wise advice on how to deal with rejection:

"I would say the more no's you get in life, the closer you get to a yes. You could be as good a dancer as Michael Jackson and you're not always going to be right for certain things. So whenever you walk into a room, give the best that you can so that people will remember you for other things that come up."

On Fellow Musicians

Defending X Factor contestants Rylan Clark and Christopher Maloney, JLS voiced their opinions and showed their compassionate nature, with Marvin giving the following quote:

"One thing I don't like is the witch hunt with Chris and Rylan. I think it's unfair. Those guys, all they did was enter a competition to try and change their lives and get exposure."

"It's not their fault they're still here. People are voting for them. Everyone says this thing about a 'fix'."

He continued: "when people say it's a fix I don't understand what they mean. It's ridiculous. I think if something was a fix the favourite would win. It doesn't make sense to me. It's unfair that they're getting death threats and bad press and things like that. I think it's really bad."

"They're just two guys that wanted to enter a competition like we did. Like Leona Lewis did. Like One Direction did."

(Source: www.heatworld.com)

The A-Z of JLS

A Alexandra Burke – the artist who beat the boys on the X Factor.

B BRIT Awards – at the 2010 BRIT awards the guys picked up British Breakthrough and British Single for 'Beat Again'.

C Condom – JLS have a condom range called "Just Love Safe" to promote safe sex.

D Documentary – JLS have had two TV shows. The first was a documentary called 'JLS Revealed'.

E 'Everybody in Love' and 'Beat Again' were JLS` first singles.

F Follow – JLS` official twitter page is @JLSOfficial.

G Glitzy Ritzy – One of Oritsé's nicknames at school.

H Holby City – Marvin starred in the UK hospital series between the ages of 13 and 16.

I Inches – Aston Merrygold is approx. 65 inches tall.

J Jive – JLS signed up to Jive Records (US) in 2010 and released their first US single, 'Everybody in Love'.

K K-Club – Marvin appeared in this children's programme at the age of 14 aimed at helping people with computers.

L Lad – JLS stands for Jack the Lad Swing.

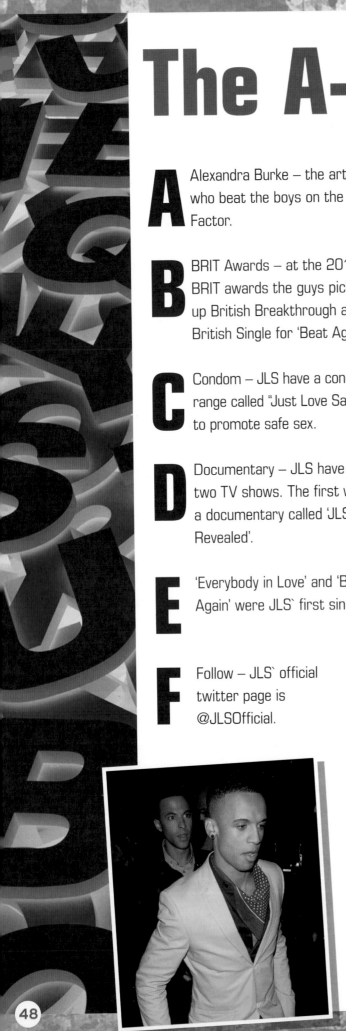

M Michael Jackson – Aston appeared as an extra at the age of 14 alongside Michael Jackson.

N Nice – So many people comment on just how nice these guys are. I'm sure you agree!

O Oritsé – Oritsé wrote the song 'Wow Oh Wow' for Jedward..

P Piano – J.B. plays the Piano and the Flute.

Q Quirky – Aston played a quirky prank on good friend Olly Murs, pretending to be injured after a fake human cannonball stunt.

R Robbie Williams – Aston shares a birthday with Robbie Williams (13th February)

S Split – JLS split up on April 24th 2013.

T Twitter – The boys have over 1 million followers on Twitter and over 1.9 million likes on Facebook.

U UFO – JLS were originally called UFO (Unique, Famous, Outrageous) but later changed it down to a name clash.

V Victory – J.B. won the Christmas Special of Strictly Come Dancing with dancer Ola Jordan.

W Worldwide – JLS have sold more than 10 million records worldwide

X X Factor – JLS came second in the 2008 X Factor.

Y Young – J.B. studied at the Centre for Young Musicians.

Z Jay Z – Jay Z claimed that the boys would become as big as 'N Sync'.

Hitting The Headlines

They may have split up, but JLS have still been making headlines for the past year of their career. Re-live some of the most recent top stories and latest news from their career below.

High Flyer Aston!

Aston began making headlines in 2013 when around ten days after the band announced they were to split, he was seen out and about in LA in an open top Mustang. Newspapers began reporting that the star was all set to move out there and that he was already house hunting and putting together all of his influential contacts in the business, in a bid to become a producer in good old LA-LA Land!

Aston commented to various interviewers shortly after, that he had no immediate intentions of heading over to the US, insisting that he'd first like to relax and take some time off before pursuing his various acting and musical dreams. He seems to know LA really well though and is no stranger to the music scene over there so the future definitely looks bright.

Don't write us off just yet!

With news of the JLS split domineering most of the headlines, J.B. spoke exclusively to Capital FM at the BT Sports Industry Awards in 2013 to say that there was still much more to come from them during the year and that JLS fans still had plenty to look forward to from the band! He told Capital:

"Everyone's saying [we're] not doing anything anymore and I'm like, 'come on, we are!'," He continued: "We're still doing what we're doing; it's business as usual up to the end of the year.

"We're got a tour coming up as you know, obviously we've got our 'Greatest Hits' as well, possibly a new single that you guys I'm sure will be playing".

City of Los Angeles

Oritsé the family man!

Oritsé made headlines in April 2013 when he revealed that he had used his money to help put his brothers through university.

"I've put my younger brother through university. He's just graduated from Brunel and the other brother graduated from the University of Westminster in biomedical sciences." Continuing to add how important his family are to him, he gushed "Everything I do, I do for my family."

(Source: uk.omg.heatworld.com)

LOVE is in the air with JLS 2013 Fragrance launch!

The boys had a very eventful and hectic 2013 but that didn't stop them from making headlines when they released their second fragrance 'Love' just in time for Valentine's Day!

With their first fragrance 'Kiss' having sold out in record time, JLS just had to come back with a second offering for fragrance fanatics and fans of the band everywhere. The hot pink bottle containing a perfume fragranced with hints of jasmine, white tea, pink orchid, and orange-blossom was revealed at an exclusive launch at One Mayfair in central London.

JLS Attend Downing Street Tea Party!

JLS were one of many bands who made headlines in May 2013 when they attended a Rays of Sunshine children's charity event in Downing Street, London. The charity tea party was held at the Chancellor of the Exchequer George Osborne's Downing Street home.

Aston called the day "amazing!" and emotionally recalled: "What makes Rays of Sunshine so special is the fact that we've met so many kids over the years. You're always meeting new kids and it's amazing when they're recovering and getting better. You do hear some terrifying stories but we see them over and over again (at events and) you actually get to see their journey and see them recuperate."

(Source: itv.com/daybreak)

Discography

ALBUMS

RELEASED	ALBUM NAME	UK CHART POSITION
2009	JLS	1
2010	Outta This World	2
2011	Jukebox	2
2012	Evolution	3

SINGLES

RELEASED	SINGLE NAME	UK CHART POSITION
2009	Beat Again	1
2009	Everybody In Love	1
2010	One Shot	6
2010	The Club Is Alive	1
2010	Love You More	1
2011	Eyes Wide Shut Feat. Tinie Tempah	8
2011	She Makes Me Wanna Feat. Dev	1
2011	Take A Chance On Me	2
2012	Do You Feel What I Feel?	16
2012	Proud	6
2012	Hottest Girl In The World	6
2012	Hold Me Down	112

AS FEATURED ARTISTS

RELEASED	ALBUM NAME	UK CHART POSITION
2008	Hero – X Factor Finalists	1
2010	Everybody Hurts – Helping Haiti	1
2011	Wishing On A Star – X Factor Finalists	1

COMPILATION ALBUMS

RELEASED	NAME	UK CHART POSITION
November 2013	Goodbye: The Greatest Hits	TBC

Future Focus

Even though JLS have made the decision to split up as a group, there's still bound to be plenty more to look forward to from our favourite JLS boys throughout the rest of their individual careers. Here are a few possible things that we might see happen in the future one day.

Marvin – Reality TV and Radio DJ Career

The boys are friends with a lot of reality TV stars and famous faces from the entertainment industry and their career began on The X Factor, so it stands to reason that maybe one day we might see one or all of the boys on another reality TV show like I'm a Celebrity Get Me out of Here or Celebrity Big Brother.

In a recent interview with comedian Alan Carr, Marvin actually stunned the audience by saying "I might do I'm A Celebrity. I like the show." So who knows!

Marvin is also a DJ on Capital FM and is keen to continue with DJ'ing as part of his solo career. He also dreams of having his very own radio show one day.

Aston – Career Changes

Aston Merrygold has always had plenty of influential contacts in the US. When the band first spilt up, he was rumoured to be moving to America to work with Chris Brown and to produce music. Aston commented on ITV's Daybreak during an interview to say:

"I'm kind of taking a little bit of time out. I think because obviously the big announcement was hard and it was quite shocking for a lot of people so it was kind of like, get away and let everything die down a little bit and recuperate.

"I'm just going to take some time, the options are open which is nice. It's always good I suppose to be in this position of looking on

the outside in and just seeing exactly what the path is I'm going to take."

So whilst there don't seem to be any immediate plans to head to the US just yet, there's nothing to rule it out as a potential move one day. Aston is also keen to pursue a career in acting one day and has said that he might consider auditioning for roles in movies or sitcoms!

Oritsé – The next Simon Cowell?

Oritsé could one day be the big-wig who tracks down new and exciting talent from around the world! He's been quoted as saying "I'm looking at doing various TV projects as well as music projects. I have my own company, O Street Entertainment. I've never really talked about it because it's not a vanity thing for me; it's something I'm passionate about."

(Source: heatworld.com)

"I'm very inspired by people like Jay-Z and P Diddy. Berry Gordy, the founder of Motown Records, is another huge inspiration."

J.B. – Farming Fanatic

One of the first things that J.B. reportedly got stuck in to after announcing the split from JLS was to start putting the wheels in motion to make more time for his love of farming.

He was quoted on heatworld.com as saying:

"I'm just focusing this year on the farm. I'm in the middle of trying to set up a place in Scotland deer farming. The farm for me is an ongoing thing. It's an investment. It's something that's different and close to my heart. My dad's involved in it with me, so I guess it's a father and son thing that we can get stuck into."

So it looks as though the JLS boys all want very different things, we'll have to wait and see what they really get up to in the not-so-distant future. Keep your eyes peeled JLSters as there's no way that these guys are going to fade into the background quietly.

Message Board

Many hearts were broken to hear of the boys' decision to go their separate ways. JLS' fans have always been a number one priority and even through the tears, fans from all over the country have been leaving messages of support and love. Here are just a few and a chance to leave yours too.

Thank you for the music and moves! Love TJ, Edinburgh

They say all good things come to an end, this is definitely the case here. Sad times ☹ Maria, Dublin

I love you, I love you, I love you, I love you! Jenny, Edinburgh

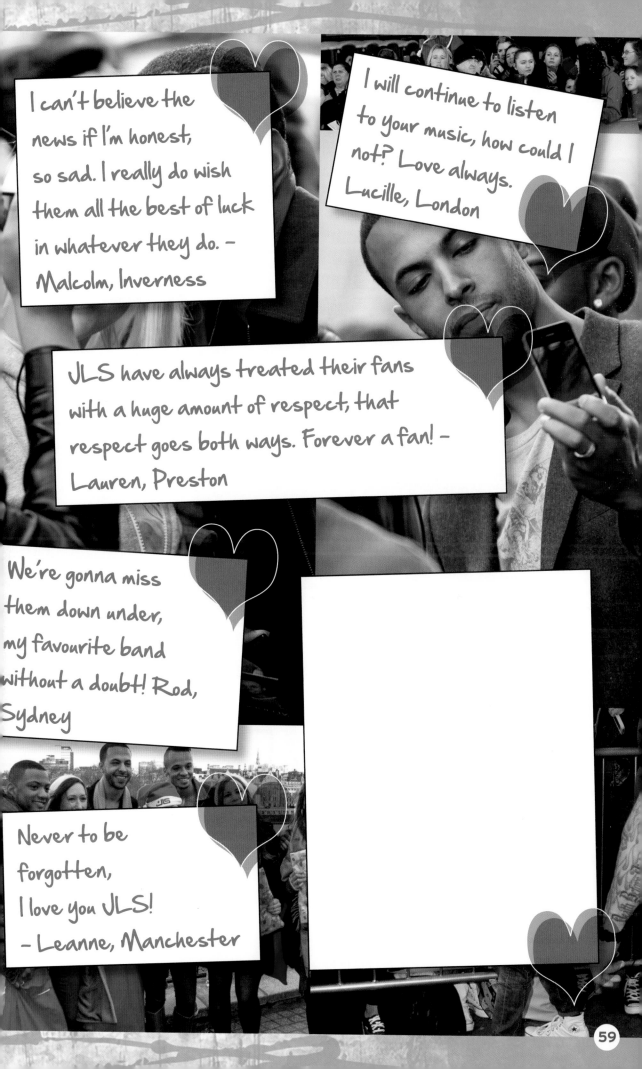

I can't believe the news if I'm honest, so sad. I really do wish them all the best of luck in whatever they do. – Malcolm, Inverness

I will continue to listen to your music, how could I not? Love always. Lucille, London

JLS have always treated their fans with a huge amount of respect, that respect goes both ways. Forever a fan! – Lauren, Preston

We're gonna miss them down under, my favourite band without a doubt! Rod, Sydney

Never to be forgotten, I love you JLS! – Leanne, Manchester

Quiz Answers

Page 30 – Spot the differnce

Page 31 – Desert Island Demands!

iPad, blackberry, tool and utility kit
– Aston

iPad, a compass, trilby.
– Oritsé

iPod, headphones, sun tan lotion
– J.B.

iPad, peri peri sauce, fishing net
– Marvin

Page 41 – Who Bought What?

Backstreet Boys
'Backstreets Back' – J.B.

Michael Jackson 'Bad'– Marvin

Usher 'My Way' – Aston

Sisqo 'Unleash the Dragon' – Oritsé

Page 34 – Quickfire Lyrics Quiz

1. "cause when you left me it stopped"
2. "stuck in a moment"
3. "something I could do"
4. " you'll come back to me"
5. "moment or two"
6. "you're leaving now"
7. "there is no gravity"
8. "flowers and the love notes"
9. "somebody cool me off"
10. "hard to keep going"
11. "drink in your cup"
12. "move this mountain"
13. "something in my heart"
14. "I made up my mind"
15. "energy got me racing"

Page 45 – Mega Quiz

1. Jack the Lad Swing
2. Season five
3. Alexandra Burke
4. 'Love you more'
5. Jedward
6. 'Wow oh wow'
7. Holby City
8. Rochelle from The Saturdays
9. Strictly Come Dancing
10. Peterborough
11. Unique Famous Outrageous
12. Tinie Tempah
13. 'Jukebox'
14. Release a 3D film
15. 2KX
16. Kiss
17. Oritsé
18. Aston
19. 24th April 2013
20. 'Beat Again' and 'Everybody in Love'

Page 40 – Wordsearch

F	S	T	I	H	T	S	E	T	A	E	R	G	W	T	V	X	H
E	V	E	R	Y	B	O	D	Y	I	N	L	O	V	E	L	L	H
E	K	C	R	R	D	G	D	L	W	L	K	G	K	T	B	T	T
P	P	D	N	N	V	U	P	H	S	X	K	L	F	E	R	L	R
I	O	N	R	F	J	B	O	E	H	L	N	T	A	N	X	M	Z
C	K	R	W	A	L	M	M	R	F	H	U	T	V	N	D	B	H
B	C	W	I	R	W	U	T	R	P	H	A	E	B	J	L	Y	P
P	L	K	L	T	H	A	O	K	S	G	Y	P	C	T	R	H	P
J	H	Q	H	N	S	C	T	E	A	B	H	Y	V	U	O	B	D
Q	B	B	I	J	H	E	D	I	D	R	V	T	F	F	W	V	F
T	P	V	W	E	U	I	N	O	R	F	N	I	Q	O	S	B	K
C	R	J	L	C	W	K	O	T	C	B	L	R	M	T	I	M	Y
A	M	L	N	S	R	G	E	L	W	X	L	A	P	G	H	G	Y
W	E	Y	E	X	V	T	K	B	Y	B	I	H	G	P	T	B	T
W	X	Y	N	K	H	L	X	R	O	Z	G	C	G	N	A	V	H
T	E	X	Y	T	J	J	Y	J	W	N	X	B	F	M	L	T	H	X
R	B	H	V	T	Y	L	W	T	D	C	J	K	L	T	N	K
P	L	R	O	T	C	A	F	X	J	K	G	P	V	C	U	N	P
A	S	T	O	N	E	V	O	L	U	T	I	O	N	F	O	J	N

Where's JLS?